C000004126

Weather Lore

Volume II

Sun, Moon & Stars

Richard Inwards

Weather Lore

A Collection of
Proverbs, Sayings & Rules
Concerning the Weather

Volume II

Sun, Moon & Stars
&
The Elements -
Sky, Air, Sound, Heat

Published in Great Britain in 2013 by
Papadakis Publisher

An imprint of New Architecture Group Limited

Kimber Studio, Winterbourne, Berkshire, RG20 8AN, UK
info@papadakis.net | www.papadakis.net

 @papadakisbooks   PapadakisPublisher

Publishing Director: Alexandra Papadakis
Design: Alexandra Papadakis
Editorial Assistant: Juliana Kassianos

First published in 1898 by Elliot Stock, 62 Paternoster Row, London

ISBN 978 1 906506 38 4

Images for this volume were taken from the publications, with the exception of those that were in the public domain:
"Autour De La Lune", "British Birds Vols I & II", "Dictionary of Gardening", "Familiar Wild Flowers", "Le
Grandes Inventions Modernes", "La Lecture en Famille", "Le Livre de la Ferme Vols I & II", "Merveilles de la
Nature", "Les Merveilles du Monde", "Old Farms, Science For All", "The Fruit Growers Guide Vols I, II &
III", "Under the Rainbow Arch", "Universal Instructor Vols I, II & III".

We gratefully acknowledge the permission granted to use these images. Every possible attempt has been
made to identify and contact copyright holders. Any errors or omissions are inadvertent and will be
corrected in subsequent editions.

A CIP catalogue of this book is available from the British Library

Printed and bound in China

Contents

Sun, Moon & Stars

The indications of coming weather presented by the sun, moon, etc., come next in order, and they refer for the most part to the weather of the day or very soon after. The sun has ever been the first authority, and has his various aspects, colours, and moods, each fitted with a real or imaginary sequence of weather. His redness on rising or setting has furnished the material for a dozen proverbs of various times and nations. The moon, too, has always had her votaries as a weather witch, and even now is not without a numerous staff of prophets ready to assert her influence over the rain and clouds.

One frequently hears of the weather altering at the "change of the moon," but careful observers have been unable to detect any real differences in the state of the air at such times. A more extended observation, however, will do the subject no harm, and may lead to the discovery of a law or the establishment of some rule on which reliance can be placed. The appearance of a halo or of a corona round the moon is regarded as an indication of wet weather, and is held to give warning as to the time when the coming change may be expected.

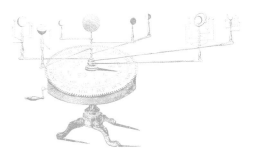

Sun

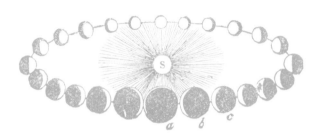

A red sun has water in his eye.

Black spots on the sun and moon indicate rain; red show wind.
- Theophrastus ("Signs, etc." J. G. Wood's Translation).

Although the sun shine, leave not thy cloak at home.
- C. Harvey.

When solar rays are visible in the air, they indicate vapour and rain to follow, and the sun is said to be "drawing water."

The pillars of light which are seen upright, and do commonly shoot and vary, are signs of cold; but both these are signs of drought.
- Bacon.

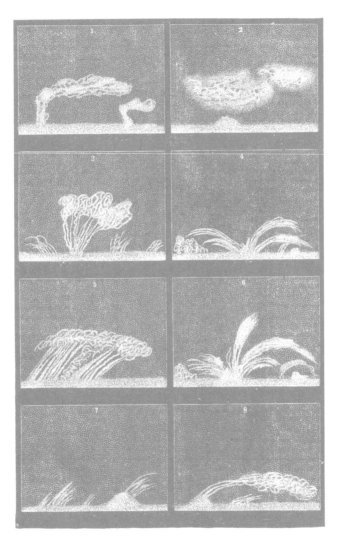

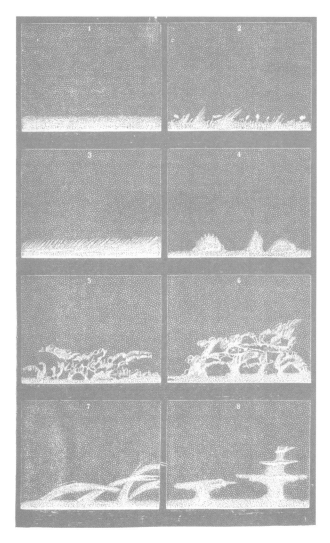

When the sun's rays are visible, the seamen say,
"The sun's getting up his back stays, and it is time
to look out for bad weather."

The sun breaking out suddenly into bright sunshine
through an otherwise stormy sky is said to be making
holes for the wind to blow through.
- Roper ("Weather Sayings").

Clouds

The sun is noted to be hotter when it shineth forth
between clouds than when the sky is open and serene.
- Bacon.

Heat

The heat or beams of the sun doth take away the smell
of flowers, specially such as are of milder odour.
- Bacon.

SUNRISE

If rays precede the sunrise,
it is a sign both of wind and rain.
- Bacon.

The morning sun never lasts the day.
- C. Harvey.

Morning

If the rising sun be encompassed with an iris or circle
of white clouds, and they equally fly away, this is a
sign of fair weather.
- Pliny.

Halo

If the sun appear concave at its rising,
the day will be windy or showery -
windy if the sun be only slightly concave,
and showery if the concavity is deep.
- Bacon.

Concave

A grey sky in the morning presages fine weather.
- Fitzroy.

Grey

If at sunrising the clouds are driven away, and retire,
as it were, to the west, this denotes fair weather.
- Pliny.

Clouds

Above the rest, the sun who never lies,
Foretells the change of weather in the skies;
For if he rise unwilling to his race,
Clouds on his brow and spots upon his face,
Or if through mists he shoot his sullen beams,
Frugal of light in loose and straggling streams,
Suspect a drizzling day and southern rain,
Fatal to fruits, and flocks, and promised grain.
- Virgil ("Georgics, Book I.", line 438).

Clouds like globes at sunrise announce clear,
sharp weather.

If at sunrise small reddish-looking clouds are seen
low on the horizon, it must not always be considered
to indicate rain. The probability of rain under these
circumstances will depend on the character of the
clouds and their height above the horizon. I have
frequently observed that if they extend 10°, rain will
follow before sunset; if 20° or 30°, rain will follow
before 2 or 3 pm; but if still higher and near the
zenith, rain will fall within three hours.
- C. L. Prince.

A high dawn indicates wind.
A low dawn indicates fair weather.
[Note. - A high dawn is when the first indications of daylight
are seen over a bank of clouds; a low dawn is when the day
breaks on or near the horizon, the first streaks of light being
very low down. - Fitzroy.]

Clouds collected near the sun at sunrise forebode a rough storm that same day; but if they are driven from the east and pass away to the west, it will be fine.
- Bacon.

If at sunrise the clouds about the sun disperse, some to the north and some to the south, though the sky round the sun itself is clear, it portends wind.
- Bacon.

If the sky at sunrise is cloudy and the clouds soon disperse, certain fine weather will follow.
- Shepherd of Banbury.

If Aurora, with half-open eyes,
And a pale, sickly cheek, salutes the skies,
How shall the vine with tender leaves defend
Her teeming clusters when the storms descend?
- Virgil.

Gloomy

Storms are said to decrease at the rising or setting of
the sun or moon.

Stormy

A general mist before the
sun rises near the full moon
presages fair weather.
- Shepherd of Banbury.

Misty

In summer time, when the sun at rising is obscured
by a mist which disperses about three hours afterwards,
expect hot and calm weather for two or three days.
- C. L. Prince.

Summer,
misty

The sun pale and (as we call it) watery at its rising
denotes rain; if it set pale, wind.
- Bacon.

Pale

If at sunrise the sun emits rays from the clouds,
the middle of his disc being concealed therein, it
indicates rain, especially if these rays break out
downwards, so as to make the sun appear bearded.
But if rays strike from the centre, or from different
parts of the sun, whilst the outer circle of his disc is
covered with clouds, there will be great storms both
of wind and rain.
- Bacon.

Rays

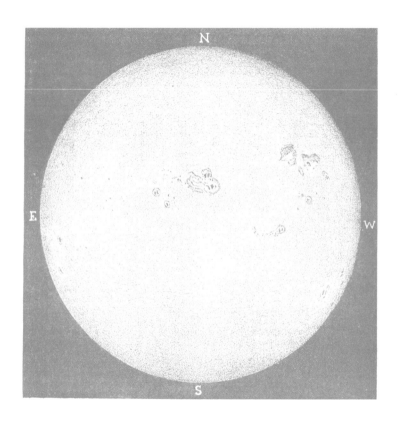

If about sunrise the rays of the sun are parted, some towards the north, some towards the south, the sun itself being between the two sets of rays, it is a sign equally of rain and wind.
- Theophrastus ("Signs, etc." J. G. Wood's Translation).

When the sun at rising assumes a reddish colour, and shortly afterwards numerous small clouds collect, the whole sky will soon become overcast, and rain may be expected in the course of a few hours.
- C. L. Prince.

Reddish

A glaring, sunny morning never comes to a good end.
- France.

Sunny

If at sunrise the clouds do not appear to surround the sun, but to press upon him from above, as if they were going to eclipse him, a wind will arise from the quarter on which the clouds incline. If this take place at noon, the wind will be accompanied by rain.
- Bacon.

Cloudy

A gaudy morning bodes a wet afternoon.

Gaudy

Red

If the clouds at sunrise be red, there will be rain the following day.

In the winter season, a red sky at sunrise foreshows steady rain on the same day. The same sign in summer betokens occasional violent showers, wind in both cases generally accompanying.

A red morn, that ever yet betokened
Wreck to the seaman, tempest to the field,
Sorrow to shepherds, woe unto the birds,
Gust and foul flaws to herdmen and to herds.
- Shakespeare.

If red the sun begin his race,
Be sure the rain will fall apace.

Ruddy

If the rays of the sun on rising are not yellow, but ruddy, it denotes rain rather than wind. The same likewise holds good of the setting. - Bacon.

But more than all the setting sun survey,
When down the steep of heaven he drives the day;
For oft we find him finishing his race,
With various colours erring on his face.
If fiery red his glowing globe descends,
High winds and furious tempests he portends;
But if his cheeks are swoln with livid blue,
He bodes wet weather by his watery hue;
If dusky spots are varied on his brow,
And streaked with red a troubled colour show,
That sullen mixture shall at once declare
Winds, rain, and storms, an elemental war.

But if with purple rays he brings the light,
And a pure heaven resigns to quiet night,
No rising winds or falling storms are nigh.
- Virgil.

Sun

Breeze

A breeze usually springs up before sunset; or if a gale is blowing, it generally subsides about that time.

Clear

Sun set in a clear,
Easterly wind's near;
Sun set in a bank,
Westerly will not lack.
- St. Andrews, Scotland.

Bright

When the sun sets bright and clear,
An easterly wind you need not fear.

Red

If the sun set with a very red eastern sky, expect wind; if red to the south-east, expect rain.

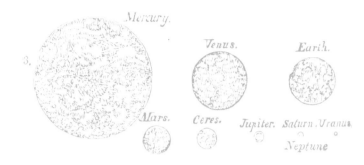

When Tottenham Wood is all on fire,
Then Tottenham Street is nought but mire.
- Middlesex.

If the body of the sun appear blood red at setting,
it forebodes high winds for many days.
- Bacon.

If the sun in red should set,   Rhyme
The next day surely will be wet;
If the sun should set in grey,
The next will be a rainy day.

The weary sun hath made a golden set,   Golden
And by the bright track of his fiery car
Gives token of a goodly day to-morrow.
- Shakespeare ("Richard III").

A bright yellow sky at sunset presages wind;   Yellow
a pale yellow, wet.
- Fitzroy.

Hazy	When the air is hazy, so that the solar light fades gradually, and looks white, rain will most certainly follow.
	In summer time, when the sun at rising is obscured by a mist which disperses about three hours afterwards, expect hot and calm weather for two or three days. - C. L. Prince.
Pale	If the sun goes pale to bed, Twill rain to-morrow, it is said.
	When the sun appears of a light pale colour, or goes down into a bank of clouds, it indicates the approach or continuance of bad weather.
Sad	When the sun sets sadly, the morning will be angry. - Zuñi Indians.
Cloudy	Black or dark clouds arising at sunset prognosticate rain, - on the same night, if they rise in the east opposite the sun; if close to the sun in the west, the next day, accompanied with wind. - Bacon.
	The sun setting behind a cloud forebodes rain the next day; but actual rain at sunset is rather a sign of wind. If the clouds appear as if they were drawn towards the sun, it denotes both wind and rain. - Bacon.
	A sunset and a cloud so black, A westerly wind ye shall not lack. - Yorkshire.

The sun setting after a fine day behind a heavy bank of clouds, with a falling barometer, is generally indicative of rain or snow, according to the season, either in the night or next morning. In winter, if there has been frost, it is often followed by thaw. Sometimes there will be a rise of temperature only, no rain falling to any amount.
- Jenyns.

Thy sun sets weeping in the lowly west,   Wet
Witnessing storms to come, woe and unrest.
- Shakespeare ("Richard II", ii. 4.)

When the sun sets, the air doth drizzle dew.   Evening dew
- Shakespeare ("Romeo and Juliet", iii. 5).

SUNRISE
AND
SUNSET
Red

The skie being red at evening,
Foreshewes a faire and cleare morning;
But if the morning riseth red,
Of wind and raine we shall be sped.
- A. Fleming.

Rose tints at sunset and grey dawn, a fine day to follow.

Sunrise full

If Phoebus rising wide and broad appear,
And as he mounts contracts his ample sphere,
Propitious sign, no rain or tempest near.
Propitious, too, if after days of rain

Sunset pale

With a pale face he seek the western main.

In the morning look toward the south-east;
In the evening look toward the north-west.
- China.

Sunset with
black cloud

If by black cloud eclipsed his orb is found
Shooting his scattered rays at random round,
Send not the traveller from thy roof away -
To-morrow shines no brighter than to-day.

Sunset clear
Crimson

If with clear face into his watery bed,
Curtained with crimson clouds around his head,
He sink, that night no rain or tempest fear;
And morrow's sun will shine serene and clear.
- Aratus (J. Lamb).

When it is evening, ye say, it will be fair weather:
for the sky is red. And in the morning, it will be foul
weather today: for the sky is red and lowring.
- Matthew xvi. 2, 3.

If when the sun begin his daily race,
Or ere he sink in ocean's cool embrace,
The rays that crown his head together bend,
And to one central point converging tend;
Or if by circling clouds he is opprest,
Hanging about him as a vapoury vest;
Or if before him mount a little cloud,
Veiling his rising beams in murky shroud -
By these forewarned, within the house remain;
Charged is the air with stores of pelting rain.
- Aratus (J. Lamb).

Sunrise or
Sunset
Rays

Clouds

Little cloud

Evening grey and morning red
Make the shepherd hang his head.

Grey and red

The evening red and the morning grey
Are the tokens of a bonnie day.
- Scotland.

Sky red in the morning
Is a sailor's sure warning;
Sky red at night
Is the sailor's delight.

A red evening and a grey morning set the pilgrim
a-walking. - Italy.

Evening red and weather fine,
Morning red, of rain's a sign. - Germany.

If the sun on rising or setting cast a lurid red light on
the sky as far as the zenith, it is a sure sign of storms
and gales of wind.

When clouds are tinged on their upper edge of a
pink or copper colour, and situated to the eastward at
sunset, or to the westward at sunrise, expect wind and
rain in about forty-eight hours - seldom much earlier.
- C. L. Prince.

Next mark the features of the God of Day;
Most certain signs to mortals they convey,
When fresh he breaks the portals of the east,

And when his wearied coursers sink to rest.
If bright he rise, from speck and tarnish clear,   Sunrise bright
Throughout the day no rain or tempest fear.
If cloudless his full orb descend at night,   Cloudless
To-morrow's sun will rise and shine as bright.
But if returning to the eastern sky,
A hollow blackness on his centre lie;   Dark cloud
Or north and south his lengthened beams extend -   Sunbeams
These signs a stormy wind or rain portend.   north and south
Observe if shorn of circling rays his head,
And o'er his face a veil of redness spread;   Red
For o'er the plains the God of Winds will sweep,
Lashing the troubled bosom of the deep.
If in a shroud of blackness he appear,   Dark
Forewarned, take heed - a drenching rain is near.
If black and red their tints together blend,   Black and red
And to his face a murky purple lend,   (purple)
Soon will the wolfish wind tempestuous howl,
And the big cloud along the welkin roll.
And weather foul expect, when thou canst trace
A baleful halo circling Phoebus' face   Solar halo
Of murky darkness, and approaching near:
If of two circles, fouler weather fear.   Double halo
Mark when from eastern wave his rays emerge,
And ere he quench them in the western surge,
If near th' horizon ruddy clouds arise,   Red clouds,
Mocking the solar orb in form and size: round
If two such satellites the sun attend,   Double round
Soon will impetuous rain from heaven descend: red clouds
If one, and north, the northern wind prevails;
If one, and south, expect the southern gales.
- Aratus (J. Lamb).

Mock suns	Mock suns predict a more or less certain change of weather. - Scotland
Mock suns and moons	Parhelia, or mock suns, and paraselenæ, or mock moons, very seldom occur, but are generally followed by fair weather, the reason for which is that they are formed when both atmospheric pressure and the elevation of the clouds are considerable. - C. L. Prince. If two parhelia occur, one towards the south, the other towards the north, with a halo round the sun, they indicate rain within a short time. - Theophrastus ("Signs, etc." J. G. Wood's Translation).
Solar halo	When the sun is in his house [halo], it will rain soon. - Zuñi Indians. If there be a ring or halo around the sun in bad weather, expect fine weather soon. A bright circle round the sun denotes a storm and cooler weather. A white ring round the sun towards sunset portends a slight gale that same night; but if the ring be dark or tawny, there will be a high wind the next day. - Bacon. If the sun or moon outshines the "brugh" (or halo), bad weather will not come.

If there be a circle round the sun at rising, expect
wind from the quarter where the circle first begins to
break; but if the whole circle disperses evenly, there
will be fine weather.
- Bacon.

The circle of the moon never filled a pond; the circle
of the sun wets a shepherd.

The bigger the ring, the nearer the wet.

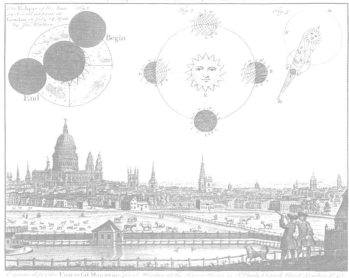

Corona

Dog* before,
you'll have no more;
Dog behind,
soon you'll find.

Eclipse

Eclipse weather is a popular term in the South of England for the weather following an eclipse of the sun or moon, and it is vulgarly esteemed tempestuous and not to be depended on by the husbandman.

Eclipses of the moon are generally attended by winds, eclipses of the sun by fair weather, but neither of them are often accompanied by rain. - Bacon.

32

* Sun dog or halo. - Shetland and Scotland generally.

The hurricane eclipse of the sun.
- Campbell.

Moon

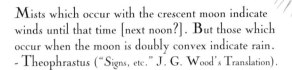

Mists which occur with the crescent moon indicate winds until that time [next noon?]. But those which occur when the moon is doubly convex indicate rain.
- Theophrastus ("Signs, etc." J. G. Wood's Translation).

A halo oft fair Cynthia's face surrounds,
With single, double, or with triple bounds:
If with one ring, and broken it appear,
Sailors, beware! the driving gale is near.
Unbroken if it vanisheth away -
Serene the air, and smooth the tranquil sea.
The double halo boisterous weather brings,
And furious tempests follow triple rings.
These signs from Cynthia's varying orb arise -
Forewarn the prudent, and direct the wise.
- Aratus (J. Lamb).

Halo

Single

Unbroken

Double
Triple

If "two" or "three" moons appear at a time (which is usually two or three days after the full), it presages great rain and wind and unseasonable weather for a long time to follow.

Mock moons

My lord, they say, five moons were seen to-night,
Four fixed; and the fifth did whirl about
The other four in wondrous motion.
- Shakespeare ("King John", iv. 2).

Moon   35

Moonlight nights have the hardest frosts.

Clear moon,
Frost soon.
- Scotland.

The moon appearing larger at sunset, and not dim,
but luminous, portends fair weather for several days.
- Bacon.

A dim or pale moon indicates rain;
a red moon indicates wind.

When the moon has a white look, or when her
outline is not very clear, rain or snow is looked for.
- Scotland.

If on her cheeks you see the maiden's blush,
The ruddy moon foreshows that winds will rush.
- Virgil.

The moon, her face if red be,
Of water speaks she.
- Zuñi Indians.

Pale moon doth rain,
Red moon doth blow,
White moon doth neither rain nor snow.
- From the Latin Proverb (Clarke, 1639).

When the moon is darkest near the horizon,
expect rain.

Influence

The labourer who believes in the influence of the moon will not fill his granary.
- Haute Loire.

Nautical

The moon scorfs (swallows) the wind.
Nautical (communicated by Dr. Barnes)

Rhyme

The moon and the weather
May change together,
But change of the moon
Does not change the weather.
If we'd no moon at all,
And that may seem strange,
We still should have weather
That's subject to change.
"Notes and Queries", September 23rd, 1882.

Great or small

Moon changed, keeps closet three days as a queen
Ere she in her prime will of any be seen:
If great she appeareth, it showereth out;
If small she appeareth, it signifies drought.
- Tusser.

Fog

A fog and a small moon
Bring an easterly wind soon. - Cornwall.

Way to wane

The three days of the change of the moon from the way to the wane we get no rain.
- United States.

Changes

If the moon changes with the wind in the east, the weather during that moon will be foul.

Moon

Five changes of the moon in one calendar month indicate cooler weather.

If the lunar period has continued rainy throughout, good weather will follow for several days, followed by another period of rain, and vice versa.
- Professor Boerne's Latin MS.

Halo

Far burr, near rain.
- Nautical.
[Note. - The farther the "burr" or halo appears from the moon, the nearer at hand is the coming rain.]

Circle* near, water far;
Circle far, water near.
- Italy.

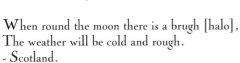

A far brugh, a near storm.
- Scotch.
[Meaning, A "distant" halo round the moon,
a storm near at hand.]

When round the moon there is a brugh [halo],
The weather will be cold and rough.
- Scotland.

When the wheel is far, the storm is n'ar;
When the wheel is near, the storm is far.

The moon with a circle brings water in her beak.

The moon, if in house be, cloud it will,
rain soon will come.
- Zuñi Indians.

* Halo round moon.

Haloes round the moon, a blood-red sunset, a red
moon on her fourth rising, ... prognostics of winds.
- Bacon.

The oper. side of the halo tells the quarter from
which the wind or rain may be expected.

A halo round the moon is a sign of wind. - China.

Circles round the moon always foretell wind from the
side where they break, and a remarkable brilliancy in
any part of the circle denotes wind from that quarter.
- Bacon.

Double or treble circles round the moon foreshadow
rough and severe storms, and much more so if these
circles are not pure and entire, but spotted and broken.
- Bacon.

A circle or halo round the moon signifies rain rather than wind, unless the moon stand erect within the ring, when both are portended.
- Bacon.

For I fear a hurricane;
Last night the moon had a golden ring,
And to-night no moon we see.
- Longfellow
("Wreck of the Hesperus").

Haloes predict a storm (rain and wind, or snow and wind) at no great distance, and the open side of the halo tells the quarter from which it may be expected.
- Scotland

Timber   Among the royal ordinances of France was one directing the conservators of the forests to fell oaks only "in the wane of the moon" and "when the wind is at north."
- J. Timbs ("Things Not Generally Known").

A few days after full or new moon, changes of weather are thought more probable than at any other time.
- Scotland.

Waning   In the decay of the moon
A cloudy morning bodes a fair afternoon.

Sowe peason and beans in the wane of the moone;
Who soweth them sooner, he soweth too soone.
- Tusser.

Moon

Mr E. J. Lowe found that a red moonrise
was followed seven times out of eight by rain.
There were only eight obesrvations.

When the moon rises red and appears large,
with clouds, expect rain in twelve hours.

If she rises red, it portends wind; if reddish or dark-
coloured, rain; but neither of these portend anything
beyond the full.
- Bacon.

If the full moon rise pale, expect rain.

Pale rise

When the moon runs low, expect warm weather.

Low

When the moon runs high,
expect cool or cold weather.

High

If the moon be fair throughout and rain at the close,
the fair weather will probably return on the fourth or
fifth day.

Fair

If the moon is seen between the scud and broken
clouds during a gale, it is expected to cuff away the
bad weather.

Gale moon

A dry moon is far north and soon seen.
The farther the moon is to the south, the greater the
drought; the farther west, the greater the flood, and
the farther north-west, the greater the cold.

Dry

Pale

Therefore the moon, the governess of floods,
Pale in her anger, washes all the air,
That rheumatic diseases do abound.
- Shakespeare ("Midsummer Night's Dream").

Seen in day

When the moon is visible in the daytime, the days are relatively cool.

Frost

Frost occurring in the dark of the moon kills fruit buds and blossoms, but frost in the light of the moon will not.

Rain Moon

Confucius, the Chinese philosopher, in one of his walks advised his disciples to provide themselves with umbrellas, since, though the sky was perfectly fair, it would soon rain. This happened, and the sage said it was because he had read a verse of the "She King" to the effect that, when the moon rises in the constellation Peh, great rain may be expected.
- Chambers' Miscellany.

If at her birth, or within the first few days, the lower horn of the moon appear obscure, dark, or any way discoloured, there will be foul and stormy weather before the full. If she be discoloured in the middle, it will be stormy about the full; but if the upper horn is thus affected, about the wane.
- Bacon.

If the new moon appear with the points of the crescent turned up, the month will be dry.
If the points are turned down, it will be wet.
[Note. - About one third of the sailors believe in the direct opposite of the above. The belief is explained as follows: Firstly, if the crescent will hold water, the month will be dry; if not, it will be wet. Secondly, if the Indian hunter could hang his powder-horn on the crescent, he did so, and stayed at home, because he knew that the woods would be too dry to still hunt. If he could not hang his powder-horn upon the crescent, he put it on his shoulder and went hunting, because he knew that the woods would be wet, and that he could stalk game noiselessly.
- Major Dunwoody, U.S.]

It there be a change from continued stormy or wet to clear and dry weather at the time of a new or full moon, it will probably remain fine till the following quarter; and if it changes not then, or only for a short time, it usually lasts until the following new or full moon; and if it does not change then, or only for a very short time, it will probably remain fine and dry for four or five weeks.

If a snowstorm begins when the moon is young, it will cease at moonrise.

Misty	If mists in the new moon, rain in the old; If mists in the old moon, rain in the new. - Shepherd of Banbury.
Thaws	As many days from the first new moon, so many times will it thaw during winter.
North and south	If the new moon is far north, it will be cold for two weeks; but if far south, it will be warm.
New	New moon far in north, in summer, cool weather, in winter, cold. New moon far in the south indicates dry weather for a month.
Horns sharp or dull	A new moon with sharp horns threatens windy weather. When Luna first her scattered fear recalls, If with blunt horns she holds the dusky air, Seamen and swains predict abundant showers. - Virgil. If one horn of the moon is sharp and pointed, the other being more blunt, it rather indicates wind; but if both are so, it denotes rain. - Bacon. In winter, when the moon's horns are sharp and well defined, frost is expected. - Scotland.

If the crescent moon stands upright with a north wind blowing, west winds usually follow, and the month will continue stormy to the end.

Whenever the upper horn of the crescent moon stoops forward, north winds will prevail during the period of the new moon; but when the lower horn comes forward, south winds will prevail. But if it is upright, or only very slightly inclined, it is usually stormy till the fourth day; or if the disc of the moon is plainly visible, then until the first quarter. When hazy it indicates rain; but when fiery, wind.
- Theophrastus ("Signs, etc." J. G. Wood's Translation).

New

If the points of a new moon are up, then, as a rule, no rain will fall that quarter of the moon; a dull, pale moon, dry, with halo, indicates poor crops. In the planting season no grain must be planted when halo is around the moon.
- Apache Indians.

Bright

A uniform brightness in the sky at the new moon, or the fourth rising, presages fair weather for many days. If the sky is uniformly overcast, it denotes rain. If irregularly overcast, wind from the quarter where it is overcast. But if it suddenly becomes overcast without cloud or fog, so as to dull the brightness of the stars, rough and serious storms are imminent.
- Bacon.

Erect

An erect moon is almost always threatening and unfavourable, but principally denotes wind.
If, however, she appear with blunt or shortened horns, it is rather a sign of rain.
- Bacon.

If the new moon be upright until the fourth day, or the whole disc be plainly visible, there will be stormy weather until the first quarter.
- Theophrastus ("Signs, etc." J. G. Wood's Translation).

Moon on her back

People speak of the new moon lying on her back or being ill made as a prognostic of wet weather.

If the moon is on its back in the third quarter, it is a sign of rain.

New moon on its back indicates wind;
standing on its point indicates rain in summer
and snow in winter.
- Dr. John Menual.

The bonnie moon is on her back;
Mend your shoes and sort your thack [thatch].

When the moon lies on her back,
Then the sou'-west wind will crack;
When she rises up and nods,
Then north-easters dry the sods.
Reviewer in Symons' Meteorological Magazine,
September, 1867.

When the new moon lies on her back,
She sucks the wet into her lap.
- Ellesmere.

It is sure to be a dry moon if it lies on its back, so
that you can hang your hat on its horns.
- Welsh Border.

When first the moon appears, if then she shrouds
Her silver crescent tipped with sable clouds,
Conclude she bodes a tempest on the main,

And brews for fields impetuous floods of rain;
Or if her face with fiery flushings glow,
Expect the rattling winds aloft to blow;
But four nights old (for that's the surest sign)
With sharpened horns, if glorious then she shine,
Next day, nor only that, but all the moon,
Till her revolving race be wholly run,
Are void of tempests both by land and sea.
- Virgil.

Changes   When changes of the moon occur in the morning,
expect rain.

Moon changing in morning indicates warm weather;
in the evening, cold weather.

If the moon is rainy throughout, it will be clear at
the change, and perhaps the rain will return a few
days after.

If the moon change on a Sunday, there will be
a flood before the month is out.
- Worcestershire.

A Wednesday's change is bad.
- North Italy.

A Friday's moon
Is a month too soon. - Sussex.

A Saturday moon,
If it comes once in seven years,
comes once too soon.

Saturday's moon and Sunday's prime
Ance is aneugh in seven years' time.
- Scotland.

Saturday's change and Sunday's full
Never brought good and never wull.
- Norfolk.

A Saturday's change and a Sunday's full moon
Once in seven years is once too soon.

A Saturday's change and a Sunday's full
Comes too soon whene'er it wull.
- Dorset.

If the moon on a Saturday be new or full,
There always was rain, and there always wull.
- Worcestershire.

If the new moon, first quarter, full moon, or last quarter, occur between the following hours, the weather here stated is said to follow:

In summer between:

12 and 2 a.m.	Fair.
2 and 4 a.m.	Cold and showers.
4 and 6 a.m.	Rain.
6 and 8 a.m.	Wind and rain.
8 and 10 a.m.	Changeable.
10 and 12 a.m.	Frequent showers.
12 and 2 p.m.	Very rainy.
2 and 4 p.m.	Changeable.
4 and 6 p.m.	Fair.
6 and 8 p.m.	Fair, if wind N.W.
8 and 10 p.m.	Rainy, if wind S. or S.W.
10 and 12 p.m.	Fair.

In winter between:

12 and 2 a.m.	Frost, unless wind S.W.
2 and 4 a.m.	Snow and stormy.
4 and 6 a.m.	Rain.
6 and 8 a.m.	Stormy.
8 and 10 a.m.	Cold rain, if wind W.
10 and 12 a.m.	Cold and high wind.
12 and 2 p.m.	Snow and rain.
2 and 4 p.m.	Fair and mild.
4 and 6 p.m.	Fair.
6 and 8 p.m.	Fair and frosty, if wind N.E. or N.
8 and 10 p.m.	Rain or snow, if wind S. or S.W.
10 and 12 p.m.	Fair and frosty.

- United States.

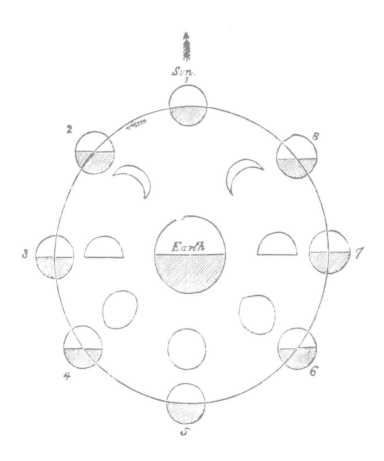

The nearer to twelve in the afternoon, the drier the moon. The nearer to twelve in the forenoon, the wetter the moon.
- Herefordshire

Change of

A hundred hours after the new moon regulates the weather for the month.
- Huntingdonshire.

From the first, second, and third days of the new moon nothing is to be predicted; on the fourth there is some indication; but from the character of the fifth and sixth days the weather of the whole month may be predicted.
- Marshal Burgand's Motto.

The first and second never mind,
The third regard not much;
But as the fourth and fifth you find,
The rest will be as such.
- Huntingdonshire.

Days after
moon change

If the new moon is not visible before the fourth day,
the air will be unsettled for the whole month.
- Bacon.

Fourth day

If on her fourth day the moon is clear, with her
horns sharp, not lying entirely flat, nor standing quite
upright, but something between the two, there is a
promise mostly of fair weather till the next new moon.
- Bacon.

The prime or fourth day after the change of the moon doth most commonly determine the force and direction of the wind.
- Pliny.

The dispositions of the air are shown by the new moon, though still more on the fourth rising, as if her newness were then confirmed. But the full moon itself is a better prognostic than any of the days which succeed it. - Bacon.

As is the fourth and fifth day's weather,
So's that lunation altogether.
- From the Latin.

Fifth day

From long observation, sailors suspect storms on the fifth day of the moon.
- Bacon.

Sixth day

If the weather on the sixth day is the same as that of the fourth day of the moon, the same weather will continue during the whole moon.
- Spain. [Said to be correct nine times out of twelve.]

Late, late yestreen I saw the new moone,
Wi' the auld moone in hir arme;
And I feir, I feir, my deir mastèr,
That we will come to harme.
- Ballad of Sir Patrick Spence ("Percy Reliques").

Old

To see the old moon in the arms of the new one is a sign of bad weather to come.

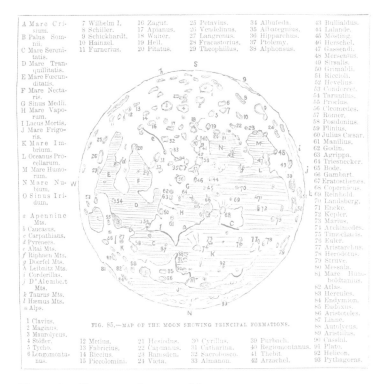

A Mare Crisium.
B Palus Somnii.
C Mare Serenitatis.
D Mare Tranquillitatis.
E Mare Fœcunditatis.
F Mare Nectaris.
G Sinus Medii.
H Mare Vaporum.
I Lacus Mortis.
J Mare Frigoris.
K Mare Imbrium.
L Oceanus Procellarum.
M Mare Humorum.
N Mare Nubium.
O Sinus Iridum.

a Apennine Mts.
b Caucasus.
c Carpathians.
d Pyrenees.
e Altai Mts.
f Riphæn Mts.
g Doerfel Mts.
h Leibnitz Mts.
i Corderillas.
j D'Alembert Mts.
k Taurus Mts.
l Hæmus Mts.
m Alps.

1 Clavius.
2 Maginus.
3 Maurolycus.
4 Stöfler.
5 Tycho.
6 Longomontanus.
7 Wilhelm I.
8 Schiller.
9 Schickhardt.
10 Hainzel.
11 Furnerius.
12 Metius.
13 Fabricius.
14 Riccius.
15 Piccolomini.
16 Zagut.
17 Apianus.
18 Walter.
19 Hell.
20 Pitatus.
21 Hesiodus.
22 Capuanus.
23 Ramsden.
24 Vieta.
25 Petavius.
26 Vendelinus.
27 Langrenus.
28 Fracastorius.
29 Theophilus.
30 Cyrillus.
31 Catharina.
32 Sacrobosco.
33 Almanon.
34 Albufeda.
35 Albategnius.
36 Hipparchus.
37 Ptolemy.
38 Alphonsus.
39 Purbach.
40 Regiomontanus.
41 Thebit.
42 Arzachel.
43 Bullialdus.
44 Lalande.
45 Mösting.
46 Herschel.
47 Gassendi.
48 Mersenius.
49 Sirsalis.
50 Grimaldi.
51 Riccioli.
52 Hevelius.
53 Condorcet.
54 Taruntius.
55 Proclus.
56 Cleomedes.
57 Römer.
58 Posidonius.
59 Plinius.
60 Julius Cæsar.
61 Manilius.
62 Godin.
63 Agrippa.
64 Triesnecker.
65 Bode.
66 Gambart.
67 Eratosthenes.
68 Copernicus.
69 Reinhold.
70 Landsberg.
71 Encke.
72 Kepler.
73 Marius.
74 Archimedes.
75 Timocharis.
76 Euler.
77 Aristarchus.
78 Herodotus.
79 Struve.
80 Messala.
81 Mare Humboldtianum.
82 Atlas.
83 Hercules.
84 Endymion.
85 Eudoxus.
86 Aristoteles.
87 Linné.
88 Autolycus.
89 Aristillus.
90 Cassini.
91 Plato.
92 Helicon.
93 Pythagoras.

FIG. 85.—MAP OF THE MOON SHOWING PRINCIPAL FORMATIONS.

To see the old moon in the arms of the new one is
reckoned a sign of fine weather, and so is the turning
up of the horns of the new moon.
- Suffolk.

[In this position it is supposed to retain the water which is
imagined to be in it. - Note by Swainson.]

Two full moons in a calendar month bring on a flood.   Full
- Bedfordshire.

The full moon eats clouds.
- Nautical.

The moon grows fat on clouds.
[Note. - The two last proverbs have arisen from a supposed
clearance of clouds which is said to take place when the full
moon rises. Close observation has, however, proved this to be
an illusion.]

The weather is generally clearer at the full than at
the other ages of the moon; but in winter the frost
then is sometimes more intense.
- Bacon.

Full moons, with regard to colours and haloes, have,
perhaps, the same prognostics as the fourth risings;
but the fulfilment is more immediate, and not so long
deferred.
- Bacon.

Acosta observes that in Peru, which is a very windy
country, there is most wind at the full moon.
- Bacon.
[Note. - There is no special prevalence of wind in Peru that I
have ever experienced. - R. I.]

In Western Kansas it is said that when the moon is
near full it never storms.

If the full moon rise red, expect wind.

The full moon brings fine weather.

When there are two full moons in one month, there are sure to be large floods.

Near full moon, a misty sunrise
Bodes fair weather and cloudless skies.

When you sow to have double flowers, let it be in the full of the moon, and as often as you transplant them, let it be in the full of the moon.
- Leonard Meager ("New Art of Gardening", 1697).

If from April 25th to 28th the full moon come with serene nights and no wind (at which times the dew commonly falls in great plenty), the ancients, from long experience, held it certain that the crops of grain would suffer.

If the moon show a silver shield,
Be not afraid to reap your field;
But if she rises haloed round,
Soon we'll tread on deluged ground.

The Michaelmas moon
Rises nine nights a' alike soon.
- Scotland.

If there be a general mist before sunrise near the full
of the moon, the weather will be fine for some days.

Threatening clouds, without rain, in old moon, Old
indicate drought.

Auld moon mist Mist
Ne'er died of thirst.

An old moon in a mist
Is worth gold in a kist [chest];
But a new moon's mist
Will ne'er lack thirst.

ASTRONOMY. Plate LXXXVI.

Fig. 205.

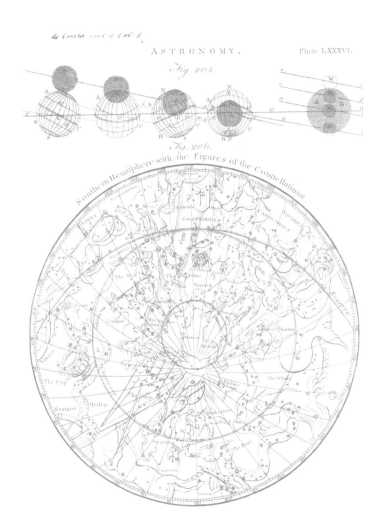

Fig. 206.

Southern Hemisphere with the Figures of the Constellations.

Stars

The obscuring of the smaller stars in a clear night is a
sign of rain.
- Wing ("Ephemeris", 1649).

When the stars begin to huddle,
The earth will soon become a puddle.

Huddling or
mistiness

Before the rising of a wind the lesser stars are not
visible even on a clear night.
- From Pliny, xviii. 80.

Wind

The stars twinkle; we cry "Wind".
- Malta.

Excessive twinkling of stars indicates heavy dews,
rain, and snow, or stormy weather in the near future.

Twinkling

When stars flicker in a dark background,
rain or snow follows soon.

When the sky seems very full of stars expect rain,
or, in winter, frost.

Sky full of
stars

If it does not rain at the rising of Sirius or Arcturus,
there will generally be rain or wind about the equinox.
- Theophrastus ("Signs, etc." J. G. Wood's Translation).

Arcturus

The prudent mariner oft marks afar
The coming tempest by Boötes' star.
- Aratus (J. Lamb).

Superstitions
respecting the
stars near the
moon

A star dogging the moon
(which is a rustic expression for a planet being
for many nights persistently near the moon)
foretells bad weather.

If a big star is dogging the moon,
wild weather may be expected.

One star ahead of the moon, towing her, and
another astern, chasing her, is a sure sign of a storm.
- Lancashire.

Stars in
moon's halo

Moon in a circle indicates storm, and number of
stars in circle the number of days before storm.

An entire circle round any planet or larger star forebodes rain; if the circle be broken, there will be wind from the quarter where it breaks. - Bacon.

Halo

If the Pleiades rise fine they set rainy,
and if they rise wet they set fine.
- Swahili Proverb.

Pleiades

Rains and showers follow upon the rising of the Pleiades and Hyades, but without wind; storms upon the rising of Orion and Arcturus. - Bacon.

Pleiades and Hyades

And when with deep-charged clouds the air's opprest,
Phatne, the spot that shines on Cancer's breast,
Attentive mark: if bright the spot appear,
Soon Phoebus smiles with face serene and clear,
Nor the returning rain and tempest fear.
- Aratus (J. Lamb).

Nebula Phatne

If the cloud (nebula) called Proesepe, or the manger, standing betwixt the Aselli,* do not appear when the air is serene and clear, it foreshows foul, cold, and winterly weather. If the northernmost of these stars be hid, great winds from the south; but the other being hid, north-east winds. - Wing (Ephemeris, 1649).

Proesepe

When the Great Bear is on this side of the North Pole, the summer is dry; if he gets on the other side, the summer is wet, especially if he be then in conjunction with Venus and Jupiter.
[This proverb is pure nonsense, as the Great Bear goes round (apparently) the North Pole every day. - R. I.]

Ursa Major

* Two stars in Cancer.

Virgo

Taurus

Sagittarius

Leo

Gemini

Aries

Capricorn

Aquarius

Stars dim

When small stars, like those called Aselli, are not visible in any part of the sky, there will be great storms and rains within a few days; but if these stars are only obscured in places, and are bright elsewhere, they denote winds only, but sooner.
- Bacon.

Cancer

Now mark where high upon the zodiac line
The stars of lustre-lacking Cancer shine.
Near to the constellation's southern bound

Nebula

Phatne, a nebulous bright spot, is found.
On either side this cloud, nor distant far,
Glitters to north and south a little star.
Though not conspicuous, yet these two are famed -

Onoi or Aselli

The Onoi by ancient sages named.
If when the sky around be bright and clear
Sudden from sight the Phatne disappear,

And the two Onoi north and south are seen
Ready to meet - no obstacle between
The welkin soon will blacken with the rain,
And torrents rush along the thirsty plain.
If black the Phatne, and the Onoi clear,
Sure sign again that drenching showers are near.
And if the northern star be lost to sight,
While still the southern glitters fair and bright,
Notus will blow. But if the southern fail,
And clear the northern, Boreas will prevail.
And as the skies above, the waves below
Signs of the rising wind and tempest show.
- Aratus (J. Lamb).

Fig. 158.

Aries. ♈	Taurus. ♉	Gemini. ♊
Cancer. ♋	Leo. ♌	Virgo. ♍
Libra. ♎	Scorpio. ♏	Sagittarius. ♐
Capricornus. ♑	Aquarius. ♒	Pices. ♓

Fig. 160.

Fig. 161.

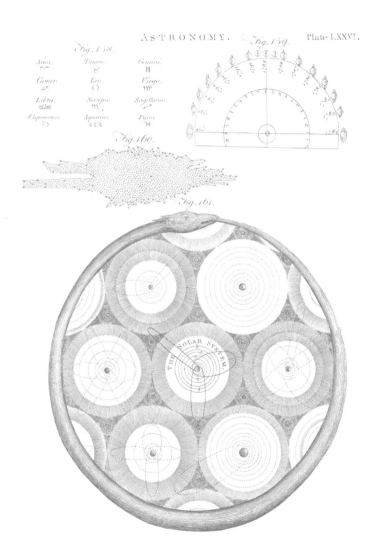

THE SOLAR SYSTEM.

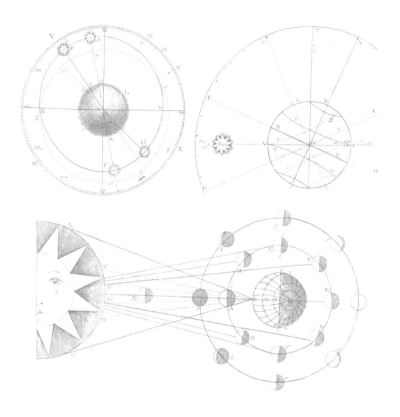

When the bright gems that night's black vault adorn
But faintly shine - of half their radiance shorn -
And not by cloud obscured or dimmed to sight
By the fine silvery veil of Cynthia's light,
But of themselves appear to faint away,
They warning give of a tempestuous day.
- Aratus (J. Lamb).

Fading

The edge of the Milky Way which is brightest
indicates the direction from which an approaching
storm will come.
- United States.

Milky Way

Wind must be expected both before and after
the conjunctions of all the other planets with one
another, except the sun; but fair weather from their
conjunctions with the sun.
- Bacon.

*Planets'
conjunctions*

When the water looks black, the Cornwall folks say
the thunder planet is about and a storm is coming.
- Communicated by Mr. Charles Shapley.

*Thunder
planet*

Mercury,
when seen in winter,
indicates cold;
in summer, heat.
- Theophrastus ("Signs, etc." J. G. Wood's Translation).

Mercury

Comets

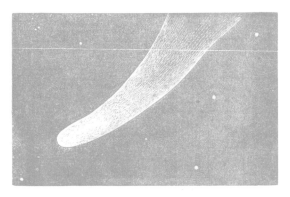

Cold   Comets are said to bring cold weather.

Wine   Comets are said to improve the grape crop; and wine produced in years when comets appear is called "comet wine." - France.

Omens   All comets evidence the approach of some calamity, such as drought, famine, war, floods, etc.
- Apache Indians.

No grateful sight to husbandmen appear
One or more comets, with their blazing hair
Forerunners of a parched and barren year.
- Aratus (J. Lamb).

If meteors shoot toward the north, expect a north wind next day.
Many shooting stars on summer nights indicate hot weather;
in winter, a thaw.

Meteors

If many meteors in summer, expect thunder.

Numerous

Many meteors presage much snow next winter.

Numerous falling stars presage wind next day.
- Scotland.

After an unusual fall of meteors, dry weather is expected.

Professor Erman, of Berlin, ascribes the spell of
cold usually felt about May 10th, and also about
August 10th, November 13th, and between
February 5th and 11th, to the meteor streams which
the earth's orbit crosses at these times.

Streams

The meteor streams of August 10th and November
13th are said to cause a lowering of temperature at
those dates over the whole surface of the globe, and
some believe that hurricanes are more probable about
these periods. - United States.

Shooting stars

Shooting stars, as they are termed, foretell immediate
winds from the quarter whence they shoot. But if
they shoot from different or contrary quarters, there
will be great storms both of wind and rain.
- Bacon.

Aurora

If an aurora appear during warm weather, cold
and cloudy weather is to follow. - Scotland.

Bright   The aurora, when very bright, indicates approaching storm.

Storm   The first great aurora, after a long tract of fine
weather in September or beginning of October, is
followed on the second day, and not till the second
day about one o'clock, on the east coast, and about
eleven o'clock in Nithsdale, by a great storm; the
next day after the aurora is fine weather.
- Professor Christison (Scotland).

Aurora

Auroræ are almost invariably followed by stormy weather in from ten to fourteen days.

Change   The aurora borealis indicates approaching change.

St. Elmo's fire   The ball of fire, called Castor by the ancients, that appears at sea, if it be single, prognosticates a severe storm, which will be much more severe if the ball does not adhere to the mast but rolls or dances about.
But if there are two of them and that, too, when the storm has increased, it is reckoned a good sign.
But if there are three of them, the storm will become more fearful.
- Bacon, from Pliny, ii. 37.

Last night I saw St. Elmo's stars,
With their glimmering lanterns all at play,
On the tops of the masts and the tips of the spars,
And I knew we should have foul weather that day.
[Also called Cuerpo Santo, Corposant, and Pey's Aunt by the fishermen.]

Fiery light on Parnassus   Thou rock irradiate with the sacred flame,
That blazing on thy awful brow
Seems double to the vale below!
- Euripides ("Phoenician Virgins". Potter's Translation)
[Note: The fire was on that head of Parnassus which was sacred to Apollo and Diana. To those below it appeared double, being divided to the eye by a pointed rock which rose before it. - Potter

Aurora

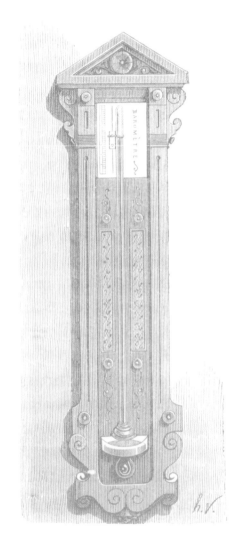

Sky

Men judge by the complexion of the sky
The state and inclination of the day.
- Shakespeare ("Richard II", iii.2).

A very clear sky without clouds is not to be trusted,   Clear
unless the barometer be high.
- Jenyns

So foul a sky clears not without a storm.   Foul
- Shakespeare ("King John").

One of the surest signs of rain with which I am   Hazy
acquainted is that of the sky assuming an almost
colourless appearance in the direction of the wind,
especially if lines of dark or muddy cirro-strati
lie above and about the horizon and the milkiness
gradually becomes muddy.
- E. J. Lowe.

If the sky is of a deep, clear blue or a sea-green   Greenish
colour near the horizon, rain will follow in showers.

In winter, when the sky at mid-day has a greenish
appearance to the east or north-east, snow and frost
are expected.
- Scotland.

When the sky in rainy weather is tinged with sea-green, the rain will increase; if with deep blue, it will be showery.
- Rev. W. Jones.

Blue space

A small cloudless place in the north-east horizon is regarded both by seamen and landsmen as a certain precursor of fine weather or a clearing up.
- Scotland.

Enough blue sky in the north-west to make a Scotchman a jacket is a sign of approaching clear weather; and the same is said satirically of a Highlandman's "breeks."

When as much blue is seen in the sky as will make a Dutchman's jacket (or a sailor's breeches), the weather will clear.

When it is bright all round it will not rain; when it is bright only overhead it will.
- China.

Clear

Clear in the south beguiled the cadger.
- Scotland.

Grey

If there be a dark grey sky with a south wind, expect frost.

Dark

If the sky become darker, without much rain, and divides into two layers of clouds, expect sudden gusts of wind.

A dark, gloomy blue sky is windy; but a light, bright blue sky indicates fine weather. When the sky is of a sickly-looking, greenish hue, wind or rain may be expected.
- Fitzroy.

From Dumfries to Gretna a lurid, yellowish sky in the east or south-east is called a Carlisle or Carle sky, and is regarded as a sure sign of rain.
- Scotland.

The Carle sky
Keeps not the head dry.

In Kincardine of Monteith, and in all that district, the reflection from the clouds of the furnaces of the Devon and Carron works (to the east) foretells rain next day.
- Scotland.

Air

Undulation

Much undulation in the air on a hot day in May or June foretells cold.
- Scotland.

Clearness

The farther the sight, the nearer the rain.
When the distant hills are more than usually distinct, rain approaches.

If the land appears dark from the sea, the wind will be from the west; if light, it will be from the south.
- Theophrastus ("Signs, etc." J. G. Wood's Translation).

The cliffs and promontories of the shore appear higher and the dimensions of all objects seem larger when the south-east wind is blowing.
- Aristotle.

Lizard Point

When the Lizard is clear,
Rain is near.
- Cornwall.

Delaware

If one can see clearly the houses and objects on the other side of the river (Delaware at Philadelphia, about three-quarters of a mile wide), it will rain before to-morrow night.
- Kalm ("Travels in North America").

Is Lundy high? It will be dry.
Is Lundy low? There will be snow.
Is Lundy plain? There will be rain.
- Boscastle, Cornwall.

Lundy Island

When the landscape looks clear, having your back
towards the sun, expect fine weather;
but when it looks clear with your face towards the sun,
expect showery, unsettled weather.
- C. L. Prince.

Clear

The unusual elevations of distant coasts, masts of
ships, etc., particularly when the refracted images
are inverted, are known to be frequent foreboders of
stormy weather.

Shipping

When the Isle of Wight is seen from Brighton or
Worthing, expect rain soon.

Isle of Wight

A mirage is followed by a rain. - New England.

Mirage

Sound

A good hearing day is a sign of wet.
There is a sound of abundance of rain.
- Elijah.

Wet

The ringing of bells is heard at a greater distance
before rain; but before wind it is heard more
unequally, the sound coming and going, as we hear it
when the wind is blowing perceptibly.
- Bacon.

Bells

A sound from the mountains, an increasing murmur
in the woods, and likewise a kind of crashing noise
in the plains, portend winds. An extraordinary
noise in the sky when there is no thunder is
principally due to winds.
- Bacon.

In air

A sound in air presaged approaching rain,
And beasts to covert scud across the plain.
- Thomas Parnell.

Air

The shores sounding in a calm, and the sea beating
with a murmur or an echo louder and clearer than
usual, are signs of wind.
- Bacon.

On shore

The calling of the sea	A murmuring or roaring noise, sometimes heard several miles inland during a calm, in the direction from which the wind is about to spring up, and is known as the calling of the sea.
St. Leonards	When the sea is heard to make a raking noise on the beach in the bay to the west of St. Leonard's, the fishermen say they "hear the Bulverhythe bells," and this is held to be a sure sign of bad weather from the westward. In winter, during frost, it is an indication of approaching thaw. - J. Rock ("Notes and Queries", May 24, 1884).
Pons-an-dane	When Pons-an-dane calls to Lariggan river, There will be fine weather; But when Lariggan calls to Pons-an-dane, There will be rain. - Cornwall. [Note. – Streams entering the sea north-east and south-west of Penzance, about one mile and a half apart, Pons-an-dane being north-east. - Richard Edmonds ("The Land's End District", 1862).]
Rosehearty	If the "sang" of the sea is heard coming from the west by the fishermen of Rosehearty in the morning, when they get out of bed to examine the state of the weather, whether favourable or unfavourable to fishing, it is regarded as an indication of fine weather for the day, and accordingly they sometimes go farther to sea. - Walter Gregor (in "Folk-Lore Journal").
Travelling	Sound travelling far and wide, A stormy day will betide.

In Fortingal (Perthshire), if in calm weather the sound Fortingal
of the rapids on the Lyon is distinctly heard, and if
the sound descends with the stream, rainy weather is at
hand; but if the sound goes up the stream, and dies away
in the distance it is a sign of continued dry weather, or a
clearing up, if previously thick.

When the people of Monzie (Perthshire) hear the Monzie
sound of the waterfalls of Shaggie or the roar of the
distant Turret clearly and loudly, a storm is expected;
but if the sound seems to recede from the ear till it is
lost in the distance, and if the weather is thick, a
change to fair may be looked for speedily.

In the collieries about Dysart, and in some others, Dysart
it is thought by the miners that before a storm of wind
a sound not unlike that of a bagpipe or the buzz of the
bee comes from the mineral, and that previous to a
fall of rain the sound is more subdued.
- Sir A. Mitchell.

Sounds are heard with unusual clearness before a storm. Whistle
The railway whistle, for instance, seems remarkably shrill.

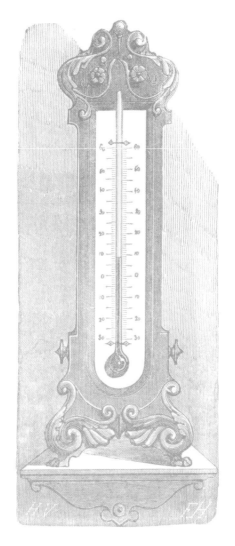

Heat

A sudden increase in the temperature of the air
sometimes denotes rain; and again a sudden change
to cold sometimes forebodes the same thing.
- Bacon.

Sudden
changes of
temperature

A sudden and extreme change of temperature of the
atmosphere, either from heat to cold, or cold to heat,
is generally followed by rain within twenty-four hours.
- Dalton.

A high temperature, with a high dew-point, and
the wind south or south-west, is likely to produce a
thunderstorm. If the mercury falls much previous
to the storm, the latter is likely to be succeeded by a
change of weather. Sometimes heavy thunderstorms
take place overhead without any fall of the mercury:
in this case a reduction of temperature does not
usually follow.
- Belville.

Temperature

Fine warm days are called "weather breeders."

What is called "foul air," accompanied by the
cheeping of small birds, foreshows a gale from the
south or south-east.
- Kintyre.

"Weather
breeders"
Damp heat

Weather Lore

A Collection of
Proverbs, Sayings & Rules
Concerning the Weather

Also in this series: